Contents

Conservative comedy

Acknowledgements

To the one who saves me from my sins, thanks to you. I could not do anything without you.

Thank you to all the men and women who are defending the truths that America was founded on. Your willingness to speak and defend the truth has been a great inspiration to me.

Finally, thank you to anyone who has purchased this book. I hope you enjoy reading it as much as I enjoyed writing it.

Trigger Warning

This book contains sarcastic language based upon facts. If you are leftist, your feelings may be hurt.

Chapter I.
Logic

I have done extensive research and have compiled all the logical reasons to place your trust in leftism. Spoiler alert: there is nothing in this book about democrats, China, COVID-19, voter fraud, or Antifa, since none of these things have anything to do with each other or leftism.

I am sure that you don't need to be convinced, since leftism is the most logical, freeing, truthful, and sustainable religion out there. However, just in case you are not "staying woke," I have added a lot of common sense to this book to help wake you up. You're welcome.

I hope you have a nice cup of vegan coffee and a few moments to enjoy this, because this book is complex.

I have compiled the data into statements of logic to make the hard data easier to understand.

So without further delay, I present to you the following sound logical reasons to place your trust in leftism:

If

you

are

an

American

that

hates

America,

then

you

should

trust

leftism.

If

Conservative comedy

you

think

hate speech

is

someone

saying

something

that

is

true,

but

you

do

not

like

Conservative comedy

the

truth,

then

you

should

trust

leftism.

Chapter II.
Freedom

America is known for many things. Things such as cowboys, baseball, guns, and pie.

If that was not enough, it is also known for a thing called freedom.

Unfortunately, there is a terrible regime in place which has been destroying freedom for women. It is the unholy patriarchy. It is truly a capital crime that women are not doing even better than they already are in America.

No worries—leftism is all about empowering women, even if those women have male sex organs.

Leftism gives you the freedom to do and say

things you are told to. Any idea, thought, letter, email, book, hat, shirt, or opinion that goes against leftism is not freedom, it is bigotry.

If you like being free to do as you're told, then you will love the following freedom-based reasons to trust leftism.

If

Conservative comedy

you

like

the

idea

of

an

indefinite

amount

of

Conservative comedy

pronouns,

Conservative comedy

then

you

should

trust

leftism.

Conservative comedy

Conservative comedy

Chapter III.

Truth

Everyone knows there is no such thing as truth objectively, not even with math. You probably think that two plus two equals four. Well, how do you know it does not equal five?

There are many lies being spread out there like socialism is bad or killing babies after their birth is wrong. You know what is wrong? Something that is just outright evil? Conservative values. People on the right cannot be trusted because they believe in evil things like capitalism and Christianity.

However, you can believe that the following reasons

to trust leftism are objectively true because no one that supports leftism lies.

If

Conservative comedy

you

think

morality

exists

Conservative comedy

without

an

objective

standard

of

Conservative comedy

good

Conservative comedy

and

evil,

then

you

should

trust

in

leftism.

Conservative comedy

Chapter IV.
Common Sense

There are many brilliant people in the world today. The truly brilliant and awake people of 2021 know that male and female are just social constructs. They know that God does not exist and that emotions are always better than facts.

If someone goes to college and gets a degree in anything, they are brilliant.

Conservative comedy

Since we all know that going to college to get a degree automatically means you are smarter than everyone else that did not attend college. We also know that going to a university guarantees that employers must give you a job. After all, it is one of your rights as a college graduate with no experience to earn the same salary as a senior employee.

Besides, colleges do not advertise degrees that have

zero utility in the American market. We know that the $50,000 to $100,000 of student loans are worth it. Especially for those critically important degrees offered in fine arts, drama, and gender studies.

Plus, if you go to a university in the United States, you are likely trusting in leftism already. Great job!

Leftism just makes sense if you let the emotions of other people be all that is

required to make
something a fact.

It is easy to understand,
but just in case you do not
see how much sense
leftism makes, I have
added more common
sense reasons to trust
leftism.

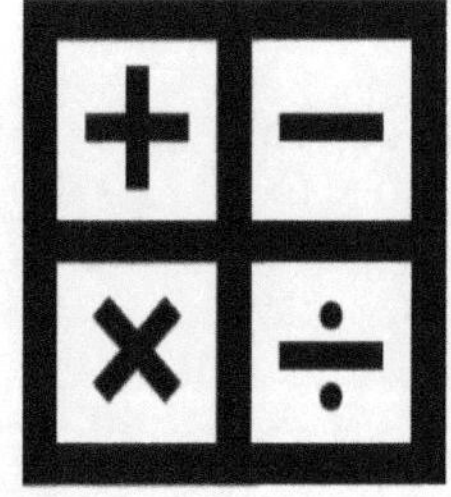

Conservative comedy

If

Conservative comedy

you

think

science

Conservative comedy

cannot

be

Conservative comedy

trusted,

except

when

it

Conservative comedy

is

used

to

Conservative comedy

defend

Conservative comedy

atheism

and

pro-choice

Conservative comedy

arguments,

Conservative comedy

then

you

should

trust

Conservative comedy

in

Conservative comedy

leftism.

Chapter V. Religion

Do not worry. If you do not like religions like Christianity, Islam, Hinduism, and Buddhism, then you will love leftism.

There is no judgement. Everything is relative, and you are free to be as spiritual but not religious as you would like.

After all, only the weak masses believe or practice a religion. Those slightly smarter than the uneducated masses worship science. Only the smartest and strongest worship pronouns and identity groups.

If you are still on the fence, look at the following reason to practice and trust leftism.

Conservative comedy

If

you

think

Conservative comedy

the

media

is

always

telling

the

truth,

then

you

Conservative comedy

should

put

your

trust

in

leftism.

Conservative comedy

Chapter VI. Economics

Money is nice to have, except when you have too much. That is a terrible thing. I am sure that you want to share your hard-earned money with strangers that have not done anything to earn it.

It is like taxes, plus additional government-mandated charity. Sounds great, doesn't it?

Conservative comedy

Besides, I am sure that you understand how dangerous capitalism is. Just think about all the harm the sales of this book will do to the broke author that created it. What a tragedy.

Even worse, I forced you to participate in the evil of capitalism by selling this book to you instead of giving it away for free. I am terrible, I know.

This is where leftism comes into play. If you think capitalism is the bane of modern western cultures, leftism has already figured out a way to fix the problem.

In this chapter, you will find the economic-based reasons to trust in leftism.

Conservative comedy

If

Conservative comedy

you

want

Conservative comedy

to

Conservative comedy

have

free

healthcare

and

unlimited

immigration,

Conservative comedy

then

you

should

trust

in

leftism.

Conservative comedy

Chapter VII. Sustainability

Well, you made it to the final chapter of this book. I know you cannot believe how I managed to densely package so much into such a small book. You're welcome.

Sustainability is all about keeping things going. It is a super important area of concern for a variety of industries and groups.

Conservative comedy

Leftism is not sustainable, but that is okay because it will just evolve into ultra-leftism. It is like leftism, plus ultra.

Some might complain. They might say that leftism and ultra-leftism are communism or Marxism.

Do not worry about them as they are probably racist, homophobic bigots. Besides, anyone that defies the almighty left will have their social media accounts censored. If those terrible people still do not keep quiet, we can just slander them with false accusations and call them Nazis or worse, Trump supporters. Yuck!

Even more disgusting than human beings that supported President Trump are people with conservative values. Those poor people just do not understand that conservative values are the worst thing on the planet today. Even if they are the foundation of the

American society, there is no need for them. After all, America is simply not sustainable with such violent and intolerant ideologies. This is where glorious leftism comes in to save us all from our horrible nation of privilege.

Leftism is a religion against violence, except when it is right. I mean, when it is against people that have ideas or views that align with the right, it is right to be violent against them.

So, enjoy the following sustainability-based reasons to place your trust in leftism.

There

are

none.

Thank you for taking the time to read this tremendously long book. I hope you found it enjoyable. If you would enjoy even more of my dry humor, let me know by emailing at J.J.Gun2021@gmail.com.

Additionally, if you enjoyed this book I would appreciate it if you would follow me on Instagram at j.jgunn.

I will be releasing much more Christian and

conservative content, including more short stories.

Finally, I want to express my deepest respect for anyone that is holding on to Christian or conservative values during these times in America. Despite the chaos of 2020 and whatever happens in 2021, hold firm to your values. My prayers and my work are for people like you.

Thank you for reading "When Things Don't Go Right."

Conservative comedy

Conservative comedy